The INSIDE GUIDE

GLOBAL GEOGRAPHY

Exploring Oceania's Geography

By Heather Smore

Cavendish Square

Published in 2026 by Cavendish Square Publishing, LLC
2544 Clinton Street Buffalo, NY 14224

Website: cavendishsq.com

Library of Congress Cataloging-in-Publication Data

Names: Smore, Heather author
Title: Exploring Oceania's geography / Heather Smore.
Description: Buffalo, New York : Cavendish Square Publishing, [2026] |
Series: The inside guide: global geography | Includes index.
Identifiers: LCCN 2025005961 | ISBN 9781502674111 library binding | ISBN 9781502674104 paperback | ISBN 9781502674128 ebook
Subjects: LCSH: Oceania–Geography–Juvenile literature | Climatic changes–Oceania–Juvenile literature
Classification: LCC DU18.5 .S66 2026 | DDC 919.5–dc23/eng/20250320
LC record available at https://lccn.loc.gov/2025005961

Editor: Katie Kawa
Designer: Deanna Lepovich

The photographs in this book are used by permission and through the courtesy of: Cover Ethan Daniels/Shutterstock.com; pp. 4, 28 (bottom right) Peter Hermes Furian/Shutterstock.com; p. 6 (top) addinia/Shutterstock.com; p. 6 (bottom) Beckygoesbackpacking/Shutterstock.com; p. 7 Alexandre.ROSA/Shutterstock.com; p. 8 Benedikt Juerges/Shutterstock.com; p. 9 Tunatura/Shutterstock.com; p. 10 Coupek Martin/Shutterstock.com; p. 12 Leandro.franco/Shutterstock.com; p. 13 Mumemories/Shutterstock.com; p. 14 Yusei/Shutterstock.com; p. 15 (top) evenfh/Shutterstock.com; p. 15 (bottom) Ryan Janssens/Shutterstock.com; p. 16 Chelsi de Cuba/Sshutterstock.com; p. 18 (top) Hans Wismeijer/Shutterstock.com; p. 18 (bottom) tunasalmon/Shutterstock.com; p. 19 Minds I/Shutterstock.com; p. 20 Robert Harding Video/Shutterstock.com; p. 21 Damsea/Shutterstock.com; p. 22 Ronnie Chua/Shutterstock.com; p. 25 (top) Engel Ching/Shutterstock.com; p. 25 (bottom) Richard A Wall/Shutterstock.com; p. 26 Lukas_Vejrik/Shutterstock.com; p. 27 Christie Cooper/Shutterstock.com; p. 28 (graphic organizer) Fireofheart/Shutterstock.com; p. 28 (top left and center) Oasis World/Shutterstock.com; p. 28 (top right) HobbitArt/Shutterstock.com; p. 28 (bottom left) pecorb/Shutterstock.com; p. 29 (left) Maxim Studio/Shutterstock.com; p. 29 (right) Yunsun_Kim/Shutterstock.com.

CPSIA compliance information: Batch #CSCSQ26: For further information contact Cavendish Square Publishing LLC at 1-877-980-4450.

Printed in the United States of America

CONTENTS

This map shows the different island groups that make up the region of Oceania.

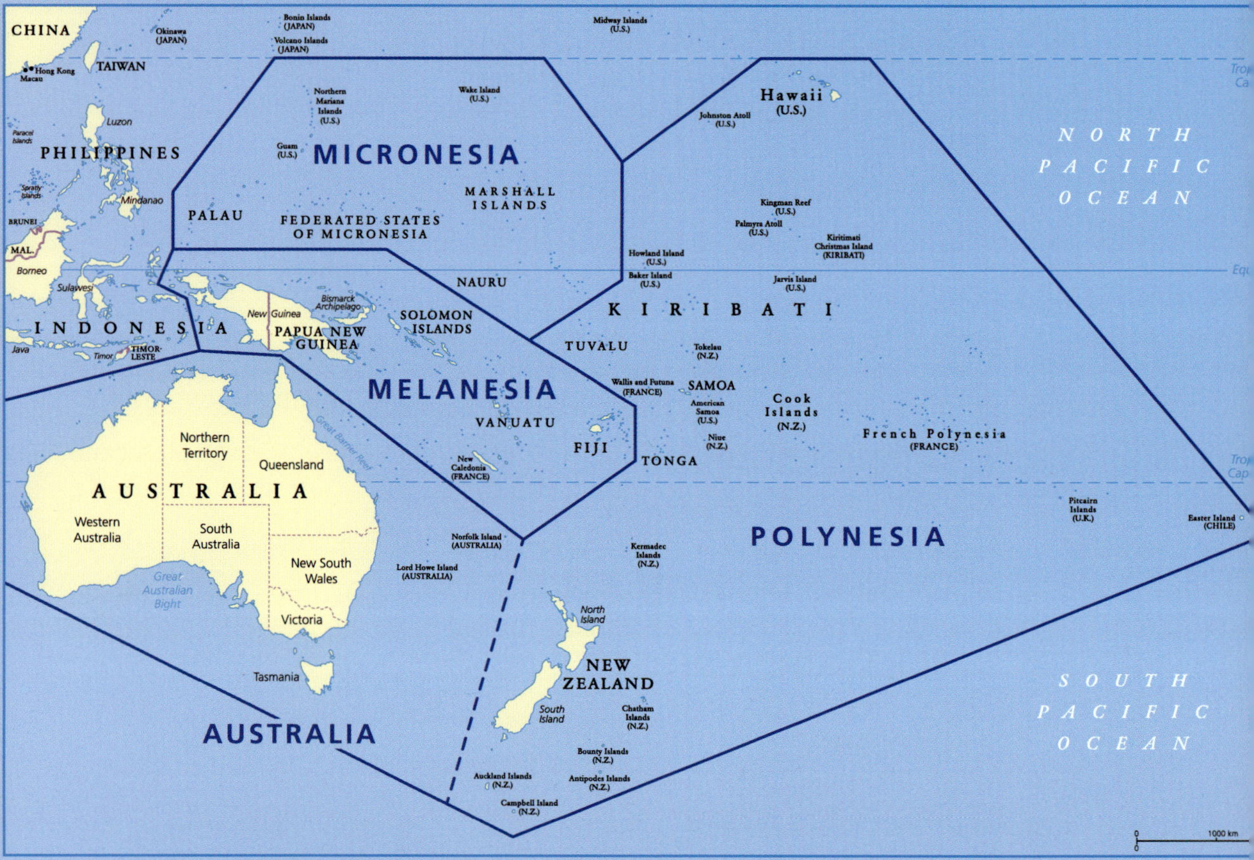

A GUIDE TO AUSTRALIA

Chapter One

Islands are important geographic features. In some cases, they're so important that they make up an entire geographic region! Oceania is a region made up of four groups of islands in the Pacific Ocean: Polynesia, Melanesia, Micronesia, and Australia.

In some parts of the world, Oceania is considered a continent. In other parts of the world, that title is given only to Australia. This island nation is a major part of the region, and its geography is unlike any other place on the planet.

The Largest Island

Australia is the largest island in Oceania, covering around 2,969,906 square miles (7,692,021.2 sq km). The geography of Australia includes rainforests and farmland, as well as deserts. **Expansive** forests can be found in Australia's northern tropical areas, east coast **subtropical** areas, and southeast temperate zones.

Fast Fact

"Australasia" is a term sometimes used to refer to the region that includes Australia and New Zealand. Depending on the source, other islands might be included too.

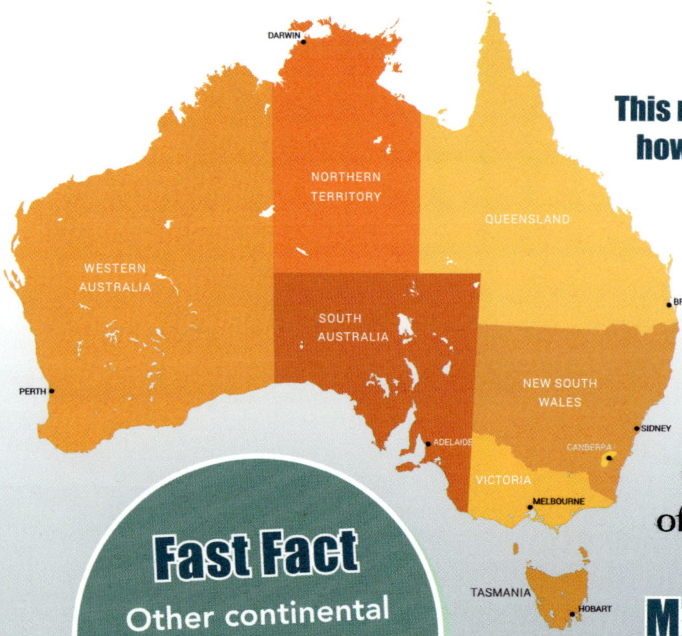

This map of Australia shows how it is divided into states.

Australia is a continental island. This is an island formed by the movement of Earth's crust that causes rising and folding of the ocean floor. Continental islands are often large and full of geographic diversity.

Fast Fact

Other continental islands in Oceania are New Zealand and New Guinea.

Major Landforms

Australia is known for its beautiful beaches, but many other landforms can be found across the country. A mountain chain called the Great Dividing Range runs along the eastern coast of Australia. The mountains are a source of water for Australia's rivers and Australia's main source of inland fresh water—the Great Artesian Basin.

Uluru, also known as Ayers Rock, is an isolated mass of weathered rock in the southwestern part of Australia's

Shown here is the monolith known as Uluru. It is very important to the Aboriginal people of Australia. These are the Indigenous people of Australia—the people whose ancestors first lived on this island before white people colonized it.

Northern Territory. At 1,142 feet (348 m) above the desert plain, it is often considered the world's largest monolith, or single large rock.

The Australian Outback

The inland areas of Australia that are mostly wilderness are collectively known as the outback. This area includes the Gibson, Great Sandy, Great Victoria, and Tanami Deserts. The Great Victoria Desert is the largest, featuring sand hills, dry salt lakes, and stony plains in western and southern Australia.

Most parts of the outback don't receive much rainfall. Some places get fewer than 6 inches (15.2 cm) of rain per year. Extreme temperatures are also common. This makes the outback a difficult place for humans to thrive, so few people live there.

The Great Barrier Reef

Australia is home to the world's largest coral reef system. The Great Barrier reef is about the size of the country of Finland, covering nearly 135,000 square miles (349,648.4 sq km).

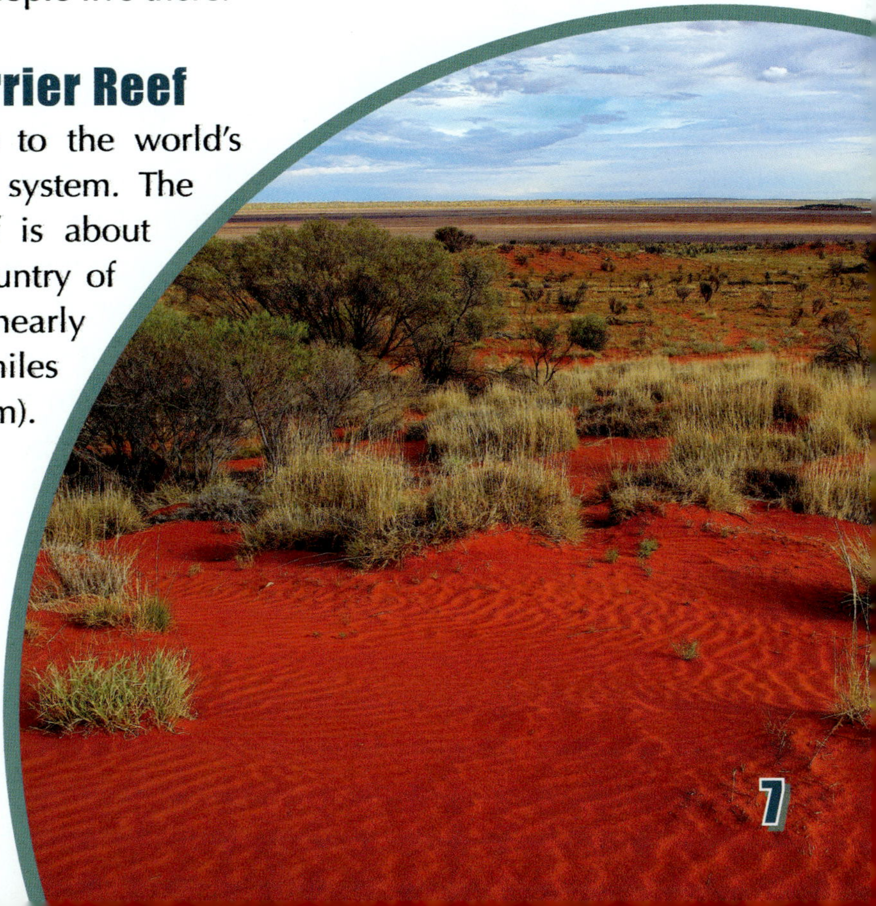

The Australian outback is known for its large areas of wild, open land.

Clown fish such as the one shown here make their home in the Great Barrier Reef.

Fast Fact

The Great Barrier reef is made up of coral polyps, which are living things. It is the largest living structure on Earth and is so large it can be seen from space!

It runs in a northwest-to-southeast direction off Australia's northeastern coast in the Coral Sea, which meets the Tasman Sea in the south.

More than 1,500 species of fish, 400 species of coral, 4,000 species of **mollusks**, and 240 bird species depend on the reef as their **habitat**. Multiple species of sea turtles live in the Great Barrier Reef as well. The Great Barrier Reef's **biodiversity** makes it one of the most famous natural sites on Earth.

CORAL REEFS AND CLIMATE CHANGE

Climate change is causing big problems for coral reefs. It makes ocean waters warmer and more acidic, which makes it more difficult for corals to complete the important natural process of calcification, or hardening. Warmer temperatures also cause corals to expel, or get rid of, the tiny creatures called algae that live in them. When corals split from these algae, they become white in a process called coral bleaching. Eventually, the coral starves to death. Groups around the world are working hard to protect coral and slow down the process of coral bleaching.

Shown here is an example of coral bleaching. Other causes of coral bleaching include water pollution and too much sunlight.

The Society Islands of French Polynesia (*shown here*) are just one archipelago, or chain of islands, found in Oceania.

PACIFIC ISLANDS

Chapter Two

Australia may be the largest island in Oceania, but it's far from the only one. The islands of Polynesia, Melanesia, and Micronesia make up the rest of Oceania, and they each have their own unique, or special, geographic features that make them fascinating places to live, visit, and study.

The Islands of Polynesia

> **Fast Fact**
>
> Oceania is home to many high islands and low islands. High islands are created through volcanic activity and have a steep peak in the center. Low islands are made up of coral and are usually just around sea level.

The islands of Polynesia form a kind of triangle shape that takes up around 800,000 square miles (2,071,990.5 sq km). The points of the triangle are Hawai'i, New Zealand, and Easter Island. In between are the islands of Tonga, Tuvalu, and Samoa, among more than 1,000 others. These islands are separated by wide areas of ocean.

The largest feature of this region is not the land itself, but the ocean between the islands. The first settlers of Polynesia formed a unique and ocean-centric

Easter Island is in the southeastern part of the Polynesian Triangle, but it is part of the South American country of Chile. It is known for its huge ancient statues, called *moai*, which are shown here.

culture. Today, many people on these islands are working to preserve this culture.

Melanesia's Many Islands

Melanesia is an arc of islands north and east of Australia and south of the **equator**. The area includes Fiji, the Solomon Islands, Vanuatu, and New Caledonia. These smaller island countries contain their own chains of islands and reefs.

New Guinea is also part of Melanesia, and it is the second-largest island in the world. Covered in tropical forests, New Guinea is rich in biodiversity. It's home to hundreds of thousands of native species of wildlife, as well as many Indigenous groups of people. This island is divided in two: The western half is part of the country of Indonesia, and the eastern half is the country of Papua New Guinea.

EXPLORING NEW ZEALAND

New Zealand is a country of mountainous islands. Its two major islands—North Island and South Island—are connected by the Cook Strait, also known as Te Moana-o-Raukawa.

The tallest mountain in the country was named Mount Cook. However, the Indigenous people of the region, called the Maori, refer to the mountain as Aoraki, so both names are now commonly used. Aoraki is just one of many mountains and volcanoes in this island nation. New Zealand is home to a number of unique animals, including many species of flightless birds, such as kiwis and penguins.

New Zealand's natural beauty has attracted many filmmakers. Popular movies shot in New Zealand include the *Lord of the Rings* films and the *Avatar* films.

Some parts of Melanesia, such as Fiji (*shown here*), have become popular places for tourists to visit.

More Island Groups

Micronesia makes up the last geographic area of Oceania. The term "Micronesia" describes both the Federated States of Micronesia and the general geographic area also **comprising** the Mariana Islands, Marshall Islands, Caroline Islands, and Kiribati. The Federated States of Micronesia include the four states of Chuuk, Kosrae, Pohnpei, and Yap.

Some Micronesian islands are actually U.S. territories. Wake Island, Guam, and the Northern Mariana Islands (including the island of Saipan) have been claimed by the United States. There are U.S. military bases on these islands.

Fast Fact

Wake Island has no permanent residents. The people on the island are only there for short-term stays.

Shown here is what a traditional house looks like on the island of Yap in the Federated States of Micronesia.

Surrounded by the Ocean

The people of the Pacific Islands have adapted to their surroundings by using the water around them for trade and travel. Ancient people created advanced methods of finding their way between the islands using things in nature such as the stars, bird flight patterns, and ocean waves. Today, boats are still a common form of transportation among the islands.

However, the ocean is not something that can mastered. In fact, it can be destructive and even deadly. Tsunamis are a threat to island countries in the Pacific Ocean. Caused by earthquakes along the ocean floor, tsunamis are huge waves that can seriously harm coastal settlements in the Pacific Islands.

Fast Fact

American Samoa is a U.S. territory in Polynesia. Hawai'i, which is also part of Polynesia, is a U.S. state.

The people of the Pacific Islands respect the power of the ocean. They know it can be beautiful but it can also be dangerous, or unsafe.

Oceania is home to many volcanoes. These geographic features represent the power of nature.

THE POWER OF NATURE

Chapter Three

Nature is powerful, and the power of the natural world is on display in a variety of ways throughout Oceania. People have benefited from this land and its resources for thousands of years. However, they have also faced the dangers of earthquakes, volcanic eruptions, and other forces of nature.

The Gifts of Nature

Oceania is rich in natural resources. Australia is the world's largest producer and exporter, or seller, of the precious stone opal, which is one of many important minerals found throughout Oceania. Iron ore, nickel, gold, diamonds, and zinc are also mined in Australia. The nation is one of the world's largest coal exporters as well.

The Pacific Islands are large exporters of palm oil, coconut oil, cocoa, coffee, and vanilla. Their forests provide timber, and their waters provide opportunities for fishing. However, **deforestation** and overfishing are major **environmental** issues in this region.

Fast Fact

Many Pacific Islands are covered in forests. However, deforestation is threatening the natural landscape in many areas, such as the Solomon Islands.

Shown here is a gold mine in Australia. Mining allows people to extract, or take, natural resources from the earth. However, it can be very harmful to the environment.

The Ring of Fire

Tectonic plates are pieces of Earth's crust that move and shift. When tectonic plates collide, mountains and volcanoes form. When tectonic plates drift apart, deep trenches form. When the plates rub or press

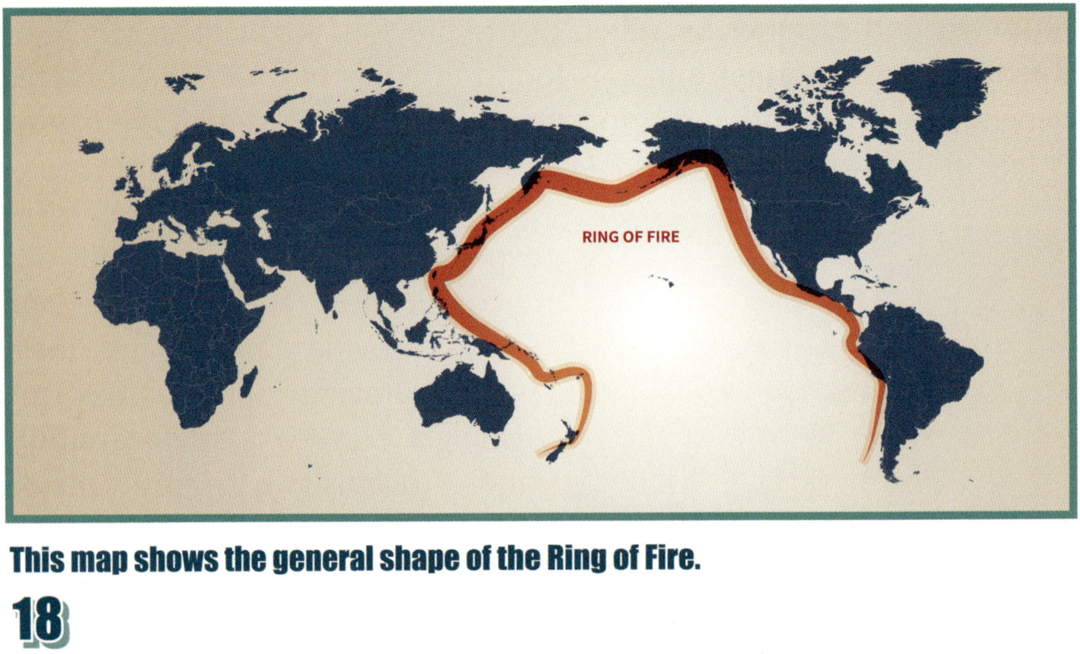

This map shows the general shape of the Ring of Fire.

against one other and then release energy, earthquakes happen. Because so many plates come together around the Pacific Ocean, this region is affected by about 75 percent of Earth's volcanoes and 90 percent of its earthquakes. It's known as the Ring of Fire.

The Ring of Fire includes many parts of Oceania, such as the Solomon Islands, Fiji, Vanuatu, and Tonga. It also includes Japan, the Philippines, the Andes Mountains of South America, and North America's West Coast.

Volcanic Activity

Volcanoes are a common feature within the Ring of Fire, but they are also found in other parts of Oceania. Active volcanoes in the region include Ambae in Vanuatu, Tinakula in the Solomon Islands, Ulawun in Papua New Guinea, and Mauna Loa in Hawai'i.

Hawai'i has many active volcanoes. A volcano known as Kīlauea began erupting continuously in 1983, but it was mostly under control until 2018. Then, lava flowed toward people's homes! The volcano also let out strands of

Kīlauea is one of the most active volcanoes on the planet, and it still erupts often.

THE TALLEST MOUNTAIN

Many people think that Mount Everest is the tallest mountain in the world, but that's only if you're measuring from sea level to peak. According to many scientists, the tallest mountain from base to peak is actually Mauna Kea in Hawai'i. From its start at the ocean floor, Mauna Kea rises up 33,497 feet (10,209.9 m) to its peak.

Other high peaks in the region of Oceania include Puncak Jaya on the island of New Guinea, Aoraki in New Zealand, and Mount Kosciuszko in Australia. The tectonic activity around the Ring of Fire led to the creation of many of the region's mountains.

Mauna Kea (*shown here*) is a dormant volcano. This means it's inactive.

volcanic glass, plumes of ash, and toxic fumes. The eruption lasted more than 4 months, damaging 700 structures.

Fast Fact

The islands that make up the state of Hawai'i were formed by volcanoes.

Diving Deep

Like mountains and volcanoes, trenches are caused by tectonic plate movement. Southeast of the Mariana Islands in Micronesia lies the Mariana Trench—the deepest known trench on Earth.

The deepest point of the Mariana Trench—Challenger Deep—is more than 36,000 feet (10,973 m) below sea level. If you put Mount Everest in the trench, it would still be thousands of feet below the water's surface. Studying such extreme depths is dangerous for humans, so there is still much that we don't know about the Mariana Trench.

Fast Fact

The Mariana Trench is more than 1,580 miles (2,540 km) long.

Trenches are most commonly found in the Pacific Ocean. Shown here is an ocean trench in French Polynesia.

People change the geography of an area when they build cities. This view of Honolulu, Hawai'i, shows the tall skyscrapers that cover the land now instead of trees.

CHANGING THE LAND

Chapter Four

The warm climate, fertile soil, and availability of water in many parts of Oceania attracted settlers—both Indigenous people and white colonizers—to this region. As they built cities, resorts, and factories, they changed the land. In some cases, these changes allowed people to work with the land and water, but in other cases, they caused problems for the natural world.

Major Cities

Oceania is a region with large stretches of untouched natural beauty, but it also has many bustling cities. Auckland, which is located on New Zealand's North Island, is one of the largest cities in the region. The major port of Waitematā Harbour is the most famous feature of this city.

Australia is one of the world's most urban countries. Nearly 90 percent of its residents live in

Fast Fact

In the late 1700s and early 1800s, Australia was a British penal colony, or a place where criminals were sent as punishment. Many people, including children, were sent to Australia for minor crimes—or simply for being poor.

COLONIZATION IN OCEANIA

For centuries, Oceania was isolated from the influence of European powers. This began to change, though, in the 1500s CE. Portuguese explorer Ferdinand Magellan was one of the first Europeans to see part of Polynesia when he spotted the Pukapuka atoll.

Many other European colonizers then followed. The major colonial powers in the region soon became England, France, Spain, and Germany. The colonizers clashed with the Indigenous people because the colonizers often tried to force new ways of life on groups who had been living in this region long before they arrived.

Fast Fact

The colonization of Australia led to cruel violence against the Aboriginal people. After the Europeans arrived, thousands of Aboriginal people died from diseases and violence.

cities. Australia's most **populous** city is Sydney, which is home to the famous Sydney Opera House, Bondi Beach, and the Sydney Harbour Bridge. Melbourne, Brisbane, and Perth are other major cities in Australia.

Negative Effects

As Oceania's cities have grown, so has pollution. This has a negative effect on the environment—from the creation of islands of floating garbage in the Pacific Ocean to the dangers of the increased use of **fossil fuels**, which play a big part in climate change.

More than 5 million people live in Sydney (*shown here*), making it the most populated city in Australia and all of Oceania.

In addition, human activity has caused Earth's ozone layer over Australia to thin. This layer blocks the sun's harmful rays. Without as much protection from the sun, Australians are at a greater risk of developing sunburns and skin **cancer**. In fact, Australia has one of the highest rates of skin cancer worldwide.

Australia's climate supports the growth of eucalyptus trees, which are home to koalas. Rising temperatures due to climate change could threaten eucalyptus forests and their furry residents.

Burning Bushfires

In some areas of Oceania, climate change is leading to more intense storms with increased flooding. In other areas, it is leading to worse droughts and increased fires. Scientists have reported that climate change is fueling more intense bushfires in Australia.

From 2019 to 2020, bushfires in Australia destroyed millions of acres of land and threatened millions of animals. Mass evacuations during this period forced residents from their homes. Firefighters tried to fight against the blaze as it worsened. Experts believe if the climate continues to become drier and hotter, bushfire seasons will be longer and more deadly.

Fast Fact

Around 3 billion animals either lost their homes or were killed in the 2019-2020 Australian bushfires.

Bushfires have always happened in the eucalyptus forests of Australia, but climate change has caused these natural occurrences to become more dangerous and deadly in recent years.

Protecting the Land

Climate change is also causing sea levels to rise worldwide, which has the potential to wipe out islands in the Pacific Ocean. Some reef islands that are part of the Solomon Islands have already been lost to rising sea levels and coastal erosion.

The dangers facing Oceania due to climate change are real and immediate. Because of this, many people in the region are working to combat climate change. Governments in Oceania are also doing their part by signing climate agreements to limit their use of fossil fuels to protect the lands of this region now and in the future.

Young people in Oceania are playing an important part in the movement to protect the environment. They have organized marches such as the one shown here to call for increased efforts in the fight against climate change.

OCEANIA BY THE NUMBERS

Largest Country (by Area)

Australia:
2,969,906 square miles
(7,692,021.2 sq km)

Most Populated Country

Australia:
27 million people

Smallest Country (by Area)

Nauru:
8 square miles
(21 sq km)

Highest Point

Puncak Jaya:
16,024 feet
(4,884 m)

Longest River

Murray River
(Australia): 1,570 miles
(2,530 km)

THINK ABOUT IT!

1. Do you think geographic features should be referred to by the names Europeans gave them or by their Indigenous names?
2. Why do you think the United States has multiple territories in the Pacific Islands?
3. Do you think tourism in Oceania is helpful or harmful for the environment?
4. What are some things you think individuals and governments could do to help combat climate change in Oceania?

GLOSSARY

biodiversity: The variety of living things in an area.

cancer: A sometimes deadly sickness in which cells grow in a way they should not, often forming tumors, or growths, that harm the body.

comprise: To be made up of.

culture: The beliefs and ways of life of a certain group of people.

deforestation: The act or result of cutting down or burning all the trees in an area.

environmental: Having to do with the natural world.

equator: The imaginary line that runs across the center of the earth, is an equal distance from the North Pole and South Pole, and splits the earth into the Northern Hemisphere and Southern Hemisphere.

expansive: Large in size and spread out.

fossil fuel: A fuel, such as coal, oil, or natural gas, that is formed in the earth from dead plants or animals.

habitat: The natural home for plants, animals, and other living things.

mollusk: An animal that has a soft body without a backbone and that generally lives in a shell.

populous: Having a large population.

subtropical: Describing a region that is very close to a tropical area.

FIND OUT MORE

Books

Brink, Tracy Vonder. *Australia*. New York, NY: Crabtree Publishing Company, 2023.

Finan, Catherine C. *Oceania*. Minneapolis, MN: Bearport Publishing, 2024.

London, Martha. *Oceania*. Lake Elmo, MN: Focus Readers, 2021.

Websites

Australia and Oceania: Physical Geography
education.nationalgeographic.org/resource/oceania-physical-geography/
National Geographic offers a helpful overview of the geography of Australia and the Pacific Islands.

Australia Country Profile
kids.nationalgeographic.com/geography/countries/article/australia
This website offers an overview of Australia's history, culture, and geography.

BBC Bitesize: The Geography of Oceania
www.bbc.co.uk/bitesize/articles/zb63r2p
Visitors to this website can learn about the major geographic features of Oceania and take a quiz to test their knowledge.

INDEX